GROUNDHOGS!

A MY INCREDIBLE WORLD PICTURE BOOK

MY INCREDIBLE WORLD

www.myincredibleworld.com

Groundhogs belong to the **rodent** family, and are the largest **ground squirrel**.

Groundhogs are native to North America, including the United States and Canada.

They are also known as woodchucks, whistle pigs, grass rats, and earth pigs!

Groundhog Day is a tradition celebrated in the United States and Canada on February 2nd.

The tradition involves predicting the weather based on if the groundhog sees its shadow!

Groundhogs are excellent burrowers and create intricate tunnel systems.

They have strong claws for digging and burrow maintenance.

Groundhogs have a special membrane (or third eyelid) that can cover their eyes.

It helps to protect their eyes from dirt and debris while digging!

Groundhogs **hibernate** during the winter months, entering a deep sleep to conserve energy.

Their heartrate can decrease from about 80 beats per minute to only 5!

Groundhogs communicate using a variety of vocalizations, including barks, chirps, and whistles.

They are usually solitary animals, except during mating season.

Mating season for groundhogs typically occurs in early spring.

Baby groundhogs are called **kits** or **chucklings**.

Groundhogs are **herbivorous**, and primarily eat plants like grasses and clover.

Their front teeth never stop growing, so they need to chew on things to keep them short!

Groundhogs are **diurnal**, meaning they are most active during the day.

They mark their territory with their scent glands.

Groundhogs use their tails for balance when standing upright on their hind legs.

Despite their rotund appearance, they are agile and can run quickly.

Groundhogs are incredible!

Made in United States
Cleveland, OH
21 April 2025

16285287R00017